ASYLUM

Poems & Memoir

Elizabeth Marino

Elizabeth Marino

VAGABOND

editor@vagabondbooks.net

Published by VAGABOND
Mark Lipman, editor

VAGABOND

Intellectual Property
Marino, Elizabeth
Asylum: Poems & Memoir
1st ed. / p.cm.

ISBN13: 978-1-936293-45-2

Made in the USA.

A handful of cabbage roses
wrapped in tin foil.

From my full heart
por mi Corazón, Chris.

TABLE OF CONTENTS

HAIKU

Breaking the surface
Something is irrupting now.
Red daisies, white clouds

ASYLUM

Another sleepless night,
and my remote
takes me to Charlie and his
blue plastic boat, shared at
St. Vincent Orphan Asylum
in Chicago. His hair was wondrously
full, and he made my belly laugh
as we waited and drifted.

The dormitory cribs were
far different from the blue vinyl
mats on the concrete floor
of the women's wing of the
shelter. Each places of shelter
and transit, an end time
at any time.

And I see these pictures
of the children stacked up like
cordwood, relatively safe
in their Texas detention camps,
compared to the Pakistani children
stacked up like cordwood
in ox carts, after a drone attack.

It is difficult to shut off
these images on the screen
of the mind's eye. The browser sticks,
and keeps refreshing itself.

In the morning
I must go out the door
and decide to be alive.

ABUNDANCE

May your house have
More than enough
Grace
To blanket your fears.

May joyful
Abundance
Plant giddy dances
In your heart.

And may you extend
Peace
To all comers
Until the final day

Of the New Year
When you wake, sated
With fresh work.

ON THE CUSP OF THE BIG MOON

We remember
that courage
is feeling fear
and acting anyway
again and again.

May you never be
a man who looks over
his shoulder, as he
goes out for cigarettes
as he closes a door.

MY MOTHER LOVED SPANISH RICE

*Always holding on, then letting go, the blood washed
cleanly into the heart, which squeezed then relaxed.*

From my fitful dream I started, as her dream continued
"Where is she?" she nearly screamed to our father
I fully wake as her spirit rose.

Her 58-year-old heart had seized, then let go.
She lay in a coma as the male nurse talked, hummed
and showed us, each movement named was respect.
Sweet lotion massaged into her skin,
as the next move would be a nursing home or home care.
She would have rubbed my skin raw
if my own life flickered beneath her hands.
I could only softly sing her goodbye.
My mother was abundant in a puny world.

◇◇◇

Her measuring cups were dusty.
On her nights off, her pots overflowed with Spanish Rice.
Enough to feed our two-flat – broom handle to ceiling.
I had officially become her daughter in 1957.
Tended through febrile convulsions and pneumonia
alcohol baths broke one snow-bound February.

A big girl, chopping her garden's green and yellow peppers
and tomatoes with her good knife, Italian or corn bread
in the oven.

My mother loved Spanish Rice.

THE OAK & THE MAPLE

for Gamaliel Ramirez & David Hernandez

In this scorched city
the maple and oak tree
grew sturdy, side by side.
Shade
and laughter, poetry
and *Borinquen* rhythms
spread near and far.

We basked in their
friendship, and ourselves
grew stronger, deeper,
richer.

The maple was felled
one Chicago winter, and now
the oak was bent on the Island
and broke.

We look in wonder
at the work left behind.
We look in wonder
at the work touched by them.

We are glad to have passed
under their giant shadows.

INDEPENDENCE DAY ON VIEQUES

The kids begged to stay up tonight;
fireworks were promised over the bay.
Bright lights shone – red, white

blue – the whoosh and crackle, release
and bloom, petals falling into the sea.
Then, the lingering stench of sulfur.

DAUGHTERS OF 1898

Puerto Rico, Cuba, the Philippines, Guam: determined,
we lived in the spaces between names. From Spanish
navy backwash to the hairy back of the United States
Protectorate of 1917, we took a step back,
as a nation non-*republica*, self-determined, living in the
spaces between, calling ourselves *Borinquen*.

We journeyed under no country's passport, named
ourselves without permission, we lived
in the spaces between. Mestizo people do not fit easy
anthropological categories – we went unnamed –
confused when choosing for ourselves a "race" on U.S.
forms. A sun people, the light ones stayed out of the sun,
as if born an Anglo Daughter of the Revolution.

We gave the world a test group for the first Pill. We
knew the power of our own fertility. Do the medical
professions insure our unborn children proper care?
Does our created knowledge shine like beacons
throughout the Academy, or are our studies the
background work for others' achievements?
Step out, daughters, step out. Endurance
can be the knife under the skirt.

BRANCHES

Fog settled on the pond. Stand
still, before running on
to the Boathouse event.
Such lovely spaces, here.
No need to run so fast.

Pop-up carts, tents, and food trucks
folded for evening along the parkways,
every manner of souvenir designed
with *El Isla Encantante's* flag.
Most handcrafted in China.

I was born in Englewood,
before we branched into Humboldt Park
and Logan Square, and out again.
Mi gente in fragments –
Dreams raised up – so many branches!

WHAT KEEPS YOU WHOLE

Keep your eye on what keeps you whole.
Deliberate distraction is everywhere.
Fixer Bannon seeded and planted
a white supremacist, compliant majority,
fascist revolt within an illegitimate administration.

Keep your eye on what keeps you whole.
The official public policy narrative changed.
The non-outlier majority is glimpsing
what was filed away and hidden
from wide media radar.

Keep your eye on what keeps you whole.
Since when is expecting good access to
basic food, housing, and clean water
extremist? Social Security? Medicare/Medicaid?
Chains pulled yet?

Keep your eye on what keeps you whole.
This is a time of change and choosing
how and when to let go. You know
the essentials that drive your life. You have
crafted your voice for years.

Keep your eye on what keeps you whole.
Forget the hipster MC who asks
if he knows you. Are you a somebody?
Forget the workers doling out a cot
and shower. Speak in monosyllables.

Keep your eye on what keeps you whole.
Sometimes you have to channel
that inner Rosalind Russell.
It's the American Way. If you don't remember her,
ask your mother.

Keep your eye on what keeps you whole.
And that neighbor, whose gentility reminds you of
Rose navigating the ice floes of the North Atlantic –
but not sharing her door –
Graciously hand over your
extra bag at the food pantry.

PASSING WINTER

for Jack Gilbert

His poems, like sleek
blossoms, every petal
and hair of a place.

LEGACY SAPLINGS
a *tanka for Japan*

Two groves – a cartographer's dream.
Your blooms – a sudden sweetness.
Here, your openhanded gifts
Thrive under our militant sun.
Cherry blossom dreams.

Cherry blossoms, heavy water
Fall from legacy saplings.
In a moment, the earth
Rose and met the sea.

Time's idea meets
Your blooms – a sudden sweetness.
Our pinks singed by snow.

Rain

for E.L.

It seems to be raining, really raining.
Feet soaked. Picket signs
curling in on themselves,
a single line of type visible.
"Don't go in!" hurled at passing drivers,
"the browns" – UPS carriers,
Teamsters. Strike veterans
"Honk! Honk!" Their wipers beat gently.
The rain came down in sheets.
The Chair declared: "Not teaching your class – no space.
Clear out now." A life in teaching reduced
like the best stock, to piled books, scratched-over paper,
a borrowed computer, and a welcome at his doorsill
to exchange some oddity of the printed word.
His own students had walked out
and joined the other side of the line.
So he gathered his day of writing,
crossed the sodden Forum to the library,
and the desk of his friend and colleague,
a worried-eyed reference librarian,
then out on the line.
His friend's former work study
fussed, brought a nice cup of tea.
She now was a new student aide,
her own job protected by union action.
The old professor settled in,
too shaken to drive home. Enough!
The indignities of his last chemo, a month ago
were enough this year.

The rain came down in sheets.
On the line, one shift was ending,
as new dry recruits arrived.
"Hey there! Any fresh signs?"
I replied, "Over here, in that trunk.
Say, what's the rest of
'We Shall Not Be Moved'?"
I turned home in my thoughts and
saved the spine of my sign
trashing the rest.
On the English/history/art history
branch of the line, people talked
but no one sang.

As Rev. Pinkney Dreams

Sleep falls hard under woolen blankets.
The day not cradled by a temporary small steel cot.
So much to set down, people to write.

The Creator finally is turned to in weariness.
Your breath? Oh yes, you feel it now.

There is that still black before the dream.
Colors so vivid, Lake Erie at dawn.
Brightly reflective. Crystal clear.

As your right hand falls from the side of your bunk
Your fingers dip into the rising water.

BLACK ICE

*"If Obama was a white man, he would not be in this
position. And if he was a woman of
any color, he would not be in this position."*

– the late Geraldine Ferraro
to the Torrance, CA *Daily Breeze*

Columbia put her arms down
allowing him to approach her.

They could be counted on, especially to bring
a tasty side dish to company socials.

Our protégés – We are proud
seeing one rise so high beneath our efforts.

The black ice – slippery, you could fall down
at the least appropriate moment.

She put her arms down
allowing him to approach her.

We're slipping and falling
on something we don't see.

Blackness is in our *Human Resources Manual*,
vol. 2, so we're covered, right?

The cow with her mouth open
keeps mooing "more." Damned if you do.

How black is Black?
Like if we didn't know somebody was Black,
are we still liable? Like if we thought somebody was just
Mexican or something?

UTILITY

The Indian film *Water* opens with a child bride,
newly widowed and sent to live among monks.
Much surface beauty – pools and waterfalls
and water poured.
The barren yet contemplative lives made my teeth ache.

What sustains us more than water?
Subcontractors profiting by 4 cents
rather than 2? South Africa, Haiti –
it could never happen here.
Cholera is for other, poorer, privatized
or disaster-prone places.
Across this country there are lead-leaching water systems
but we'll get to the infrastructure repairs. Someday.
Before another Flint or shuttered Detroit.

I can remember when we once had public utilities. Water
was one such utility, provided by our local governments,
as an essential product for our common civic life.

GAS HEATER

In the asbestos-shingled two-flat,
the central living room held
a cocoa brown gas heater,
flames flickers through
its window in front.

My left ear, still throbbed
from the Midwestern open cold.
I would draw as close
as I could to the pilot light
through its window – so quietly

so quietly, the secret
of my father's shotgun
resting in the next room.

POEM FOR VIETNAMESE REUNIFICATION DAY 2017

in reply to Đặng Thân

Must each generation
have its own war?

My birth father, a carpenter
left colonial Puerto Rico
for Chicago. When I began
to sprout from his hands and heart,
he enlisted in the U.S. Army
but never returned home.
Did he help occupy Korea?
Would he have marched for
brown and Black civil rights?
I do not know.

My adoptive father
son of Italian immigrants
was said to have served
in the Pacific Theater
during WWII, U.S. Army.
He died with his secrets and limp
shrouded in a fog of dementia.

My favorite uncle told me
stories of a wider world
and urged me to become
a part of it. He was a career
U.S. Army man, until
he came home from Vietnam
for his father's funeral
and never went back.
He kept saying
"It's a dirty dirty war"

There were questions
I could not begin to answer
as I approached my small
group of Vietnamese female
refugee students in 1976.
As a peer tutor for English and
American government, we could
only examine one phrase
and one right at a time.

My own late ex-husband enlisted
in the U.S. Air Force, and was taught to encrypt
body counts, two days before his university
reinstatement came in 1965. He would work
tirelessly for other paralyzed vets. He hated
jingoism of all kinds. His own literal
bruised spine never healed.
He never asked for what he saw
as lost: the perfect light,
the value of his kisses.

"Peace!"/Christmas Bombings '72

"Peace!"
once shouted from the housetops
and chanted in the churches,
is a single
hushed
sadly murmured
plea for sanity
Now more than ever.

LITANY FOR PEACE

Pick up a rock.
Set it down.

Pick up a rock.
Set it down.

Backs bowed.
Eyes to ground.
Set it down.

Eyes to ground becomes embers
Inflame the underbrush.
Set it down.

Lit underbrush, hot brush
Cracks open forests.
Set it down.

Across the field
We can only watch.
We each have a right to exist.

We live our lives on cold streets
Crave homes of our own. No school,
No hospital, no ministry of justice
Is impervious to flame.

Set it down. Set it down.
Set it down. NOW.

A *NEW YORKER* POEM

The wind turned everything over and over and
       down the street: the rusty beer cans, crumpled
gum wrappers,
       burnished leaves.
I expected even you to turn up eventually;
right there, a chameleon peeking out from between
       two curled leaves in Central Park.

Your letter was worn from folding and unfolding.
A line of brown after the part where you say,
"What I mean, Roberto, is...." I do not understand.
You continued in Portuguese. You know I only read French.
And my name is Bernardo.
I am no fool, Woman – I have read both *Fear of Flying*
and *Madame Bovary*, and I know how women think.

Refolding your note, I slip it into the dash
of my silver MG, expertly adjust the mirror
to be rid of the glare of the setting sun,
and drive off. I must learn to take pleasure in small things.

ON THE 36 BROADWAY BUS

"It's raining. Misting," she confirms,
the one standing to the one
sitting, plastic carefully arranged
yet spilling into the aisle.

Head slowly rises, meets
an eye of the one standing.
"It is."

The man in the too-tight brown suit steps back,
further down the aisle, allowing space while
fumbling for his personal music player, drops it,
curses softly, then finds a seat.

Everybody slightly rearranges themselves.

Memory of daybreak and fresh hot chocolate
pours into her consciousness.

She sits and smiles to herself.
The other one, sitting, nods.

CEREMONIES

I.

Never know if there is just one, and how dead it is.
Did it die a week ago, or a former tenant ago,
died somewhere else, corpse moved to beneath my refrigerator?
This shiny black and fuzzy brown beetle – not in my covered
ceramic flour or white sugar jars! It's had a life I need to know.

II.

This scarred hand of a 4-year-old neighbor trusted me. Let me
take it and hold it till his mom came downstairs, looked up
happy danced and smiled. They were going out – somewhere –
just not the apartment where his crying
bounced off of the pressing walls
and his mother's voices answered.

III.

The Blue Box key locked everything.
All the exceptions and proxies
to lead a somewhat registered voter
to casting a ballot, all the helps
in Chinese or Polish or Spanish or Bengali,
depending on the precinct;
the magnifiers or headphones or small folding chair as well.
The Blue Box key held the promise of a new beginning,
things would be done right at $170 per, this time,
between the AM pecan rolls and lunch.

FOUL FERN

"They're all out
there," she rages and she
rages from in here
to out there and they're
real because she sees
them and she sees them –
"Look! Right there!
They're coming
closer!
That Goddamnmotherfuckingcocksucker
Harry Truman!"

Foul Fern. Her red plastic sandals
down Devon Avenue.
That's her street and her
anger so hot her red
plastic sandals nearly melt. The kids
hiss and blow stage kisses.
Across the street the deli
ladies tsk tsk about that poor....
Left her cold, he did.... Hush Tommy!
And quit staring.... She
just couldn't take it....

On every corner
a fresh gust of north wind
rumples her hair,
picks at the scraps of paper
where she writes down
all the things she wants to remember
before gathering them into her pockets, picks
at the scraps of paper till
just one is tossed up
barely out of her reach.

PORNOGRAPHIC PICTURES

after the assassinations of Mr. Stephen T. Johns
and Dr. George Tiller, June 2009

We've all seen the pornographic pictures.
We've all seen what's lead to a
clothesline full of dirty laundry:
A forearm stamped up and down
with cigarette burns.

A head, bright with *chola* colors
slammed through their nursery wall.

Her own mouth,
so, so much better than his,
finally shut up – by a fist full of keys,
and a left hook from behind,
aimed repeatedly at her face.
Because, (sobbing) he was so sorry.
He could not protect her
(she – so trusting!) from that animal
who just came and took her.

We've all seen the pornographic pictures,
then locked our own deadbolts,
and turned our own pages.

We've also seen other pictures:
of lockups with cots in the halls
of children sleeping under desks
of social service offices, lacking
in emergency placements,
and homes barred from taking them back.

"Which child are you asking about?" her
hand reaching for the top of a pile
of files at the tipping point.

IN AMSTERDAM

Swaying woman with glossy black curls
Sweeps her red-lit stoop
Swinging into the shadows
Some half-remembered broken-
English blues verse.

THE DIRECT VELVET ROUTE

Troops know that the truest
way to an enemy's anguish
is through the direct velvet route
of vagina, mouth, or anus
of his wife or young daughter,
preferably in front of him.
It's a time-tested war crime, that
struggles to be named as such.

Here at home, the common
"I want some of that,"
muttered from a park bench,
or as he gets off a public bus
following a young girl.
Studies report a child-woman's
appeal peaks at age 13.
My mother once drove over
a curb as a man leached after
a neighbor's 12-year-old daughter
entering a grocery store.
Thick black-girl thighs and woman hips.
She looks so grown, she
must be grown. What child?
"I want some of this."

As pirates cruise the West Coast
of Africa, and desperate parents
take small sums to ensure
domestic training, a possible life abroad.
Hope beyond hope,
then really do not want to know,
as the dream ships sail away.

On a nice night, it would be good
to go out for a walk. I hear my own
mother's voice saying *Don't go.*
There are bad men out there.
The small woman enwrapped in
a simple green sari has been
in the States for three weeks.
A small, proud smile.
Where is Chicago? she asks.
Security finds her apartment,
and asks me to see her upstairs
to her unlocked apartment.

"Life doesn't frighten me" wrote
Maya Angelou. But it does.
Truly, it does. The detailed catalogues
of violence to girls and women
shut us down. There are no longer stages
for girls to play at future sexual selves,
to flirt in earnest without consequence.
Her gaze – direct, sure and unaffected –
laughter in her eyes.

There must be a way to slip
our fingers deep into the earth
all at once, and right its orbit.

HAIKU

Black crow, a woman.
You do not take the perfect
cabbage from her hands.

BODY LANGUAGE

after Bunuel & Dali's "Un Chen Andalou"

In his dreams
    she would find safety beside him,
would ignore the flash of
    passing strangers in darkened storefronts.

In his dreams they would
    go back to her place, turn a single lock
      enter the plush darkness of her
        apartment, and he'd easily
          draw her to him.
Without her turning quickly
    to light a small lamp, to glance
      over and through the clear vinyl shower curtain
and draw the deadbolt, pull the latch and
    slip closed the chain, giving a slight push
      for good measure.

In his dreams on this warm night
    they'd wander out onto her back porch
      her face washed in silver by the full moon.
And when he'd stroke her right cheek
    she wouldn't flinch, and when he nuzzled
      the nape of her neck, all that he'd feel
    would be the soft syllable
      "OH"
    without the slight stiffening and soft
      "shit" and sigh.
In his dreams
    he could offer her
night's endless possibilities
    and she would stroke him
till her heart was more than full.

THROUGH MY BEST FRIEND'S WINDOW

Borrowed blankets and pillows
The neglected notebook
Another squad car passed.

Two houses. Across town, my house –
Courtyard and kitchen gutted by fire
Bedroom untouched.
White sheets – so cool, so smooth.

I steal back. Spreading apart
My sheets, making room
His shoulders
Musk of smoke rose.

PERFORMANCE POET WITH DAUGHTER

for Chuck Perkins

There is something about
a tiny girl hand
wrapped around a thick
Daddy finger

Trusting him to just be there
to fix the bathroom light
the car in the dark parking lot
the leftover bit of splinter

To trust he'd lift his heart so high
her squeals bounce off the ceiling
until she's lifted down gently, onto
her toes, the wooded floor becoming carpet

A hand lifting her up, and not lingering.

Some fathers seek credit, still others are owed –
as when the back of his hand turns
palm up, and his daughter's fist
quietly, surely will open in forgiveness.

DEBRIS

"The police admitted that they were so overwhelmed by the quantity of wreckage... that their tracking and labeling practices were flawed." News item about Pan Am Flight 103, which exploded over Lockerbie, Scotland

There is, under all this, a floor.
Debris does not leach through to the basement.

I turn over layers of newsprint to reveal:
      at least one source of hairball smells
      a book loaned by a friend
      receipts from non-deductibles
      a statement of my phone activity 6 months ago
      an unanswered love letter.

I still feel the light stride
      of a cockroach tramping down my arm,
      while I dress for black tie in my sleek bronze gown.
I admit that no one
      has come through my door with a gun
            in over 20 years.
I rise to take pruning shears and a fire extinguisher
      to the very Sacred Heart of Jesus.
Touch bone, touch lock, touch floor.
It is time to sort this into refuse.

AN OTHERWISE UNEVENTFUL SUNDAY IN MARCH. CHICAGO

It looks like James Franco over in the next booth.
But it is probably just Bob Piazza, waiting for his toast.
It will just be toast, rye maybe,
but hopefully with a mixed jelly.
not a TOAST bar
awaited by local hipster swarms.
They slouch past, plaid flannel shirts and beards
waving in the breeze. Their girls struggle
to keep up, girls with double pink space buns,
baby doll dresses, leggings and biker boots.

From this side of the plate glass,
I see they put up vacancy signs in the
new development across the street.
Six new condos with oak flooring,
granite kitchens and faux fireplaces.
Black wrought iron stakes out the entrance
amidst a block of: 2-flats, a bungalow,
a retail/rental tower,
red brick, yellow brick,
and a brownstone around the corner.
The black gates, antipodes to the fence
around the West Side in 1968.
A jogger in a ski hat cuts across the street,
and is lost to a pothole/sinkhole.
The grey sky breaks open with a momentary drizzle.

The near corner reveals a defiant fist
– an Early Spring Bouquet – dodging grocery shoppers,
grim-faced, with LINK cards tucked away
– yellow and purple tulip heads bobbing
in the cool breeze. Grandchildren of Maxwell Street
vendors pass new arrivals from
O'Hare. Laborers in white T-shirts, jeans and Bears jackets
come from some third shift, eyes down.

Bob/James gets his toast. It is wheat, but he takes it anyway.
My stomach starts to growl for its
grilled cheese sandwich, tomatoes and tuna on wheat.
I would take white. My ice tea is
melting. The waffles for the neighboring booth smell
of bacon and strawberries.
The City That Works at looking like it is working.
Toronto reasonably stands in for Chicago.
Canadian school children dressed in white and blue,
carrying approved texts,
while we wage the business of education,
which is business first. Perhaps
casinos in vacant CPS school buildings,
learning being such a crap shoot.

Here is my sandwich.

Somewhere down in Uptown, that persistent beauty,
Chicago, sits down at her kitchen table
to a deep dish pie, before rising in search of a Ventra card
at the Wilson renovated elevated.

CLOSER

"Objects in mirror are closer than they appear."
We will sleep under a canopy of stars
as do the red and blue encampments.

We'll encounter each other fresh, in nature
far away from the distractions of the City.
"Objects in mirror are closer than they appear."

Do black bears smell the unwrapped coffee grounds
and bacon grease from the neighboring campsite
as do the red and blue encampments?

"For twenty dollars more, we could have gotten
an electric hookup, and be near a flush toilet."
"Objects in mirror are closer than they appear."

But we came to sleep under a canopy of stars.
That canopy now ripped open – torrents of rain
as are the red and blue encampments.

In the car heading home, only the sound of tires
hitting pavement, as the City rises into view
as do the red and blue encampments.
"Objects in mirror are closer than they appear."

*[The phrase "objects in (the) mirror are closer than they
appear" is a safety warning that is required to be
engraved on passenger side mirrors of motor vehicles in
the United States, Canada, Nepal, India, and Saudi
Arabia. Wikipedia.]*

IDYLL

after Anne Sexton

Hard to count to seven
in a fog, work and pension
     kicked out from
under, looking too pretty
to be truly needy. And besides, your cheekbones
upset the wife.

Where is the landing strip? It
used to be
     right there. To be ordinary
on a fresh day –

to stand or walk
at will, motor off
or idling.

JOEY HEATHERTON
VS. LINDSAY WAGNER

Joey, promising fitful dreams
would never, ever let us be satisfied
with a good night's sleep
on a mattress molded to the dreamer's shape.

Such sleep – predictable disturbed activity
not sleep coming from social activity.
Set it down, our mothers would have said.
Never go to bed angry.

Lindsay, remind us: What is tired?
Perhaps to be weary for a replacement partner,
with fuller lips, thicker, err, thighs.
They would approach the foot of the bed

with some indescribable possibility. Or finally
someone who always remembers to take out
the separated trash and check the locks.
Someone who distinguishes Hegel from Kant.

Someone who approaches you, knowing and
full-bodied as fresh-brewed Sumatra and milk,
poured into a favorite hand thrown mug.
Firm and sure – sure their soul was still intact.

Rue De Huchette, March 1976

From my hotel room above the Algerian restaurant, I walk down the narrow steps and out onto the side street. It is more a cleavage in heaped medieval stones than a street lined with green plate glass and *pensions*. Dawn breaks. From some shadow, an old man is touched by a fresh shaft of daylight, and begins to sweep the cobblestones with his bundled twig broom. Across the way, the *Boulangerie* is methodically opening. I could already smell the thick sweetness of crusty bread. Madame is the first shopkeeper to open her door, fling her pail of water onto the shop's stoop, and sweep the remains into the street. I continue down to the main street, past the frying Tunisian donuts with mint tea, and newly chalked daily specials written in Vietnamese/French/English, and out onto the bright boulevard. There, that man from the disco last night, brass in pocket, finally makes his way home. A massive St. Michael directs traffic. And those ubiquitous billboards: the great white shark devours the water-skier, Jack Nicholson models a straitjacket, wonder make-up for "all complexions." Thin young girls hurry past in tight jeans, cowboy boots, hennaed hair, and twelve layers of bulky sweaters.

FURROW

Many fields lie fallow, waiting.
The hand lingers over
the pulse from the rounded belly.
Even when the potential is gone
the mystery remains.

No perfect child will unfurl tiny fingers here.
It goes to the heart of who we are, and beyond.
Imaging seeks and finds
one intact ovary. The other
hides behind fists of gristle and blood.

The hand lingers over
the pulse from the rounded belly.
Belly and hand are mine. Many fields
lie fallow, waiting.
I am legion.

Of Margaret Court
and Butterfly Strokes

It should be simple, a tennis ball's arc.
Oh the rhythm of churning water
from butterfly strokes, each stroke a standard
met through the lithe flesh of a woman athlete.

Listen. They are arranging the brass now.
Purcell strains run through national anthems.
Oh Margaret Court, where did your gaze fall?
Does a simple arc sanction your deadly return?

As a girl, I was witness to your play
on the clay courts of Wimbledon, your home
hard court Australian Open, your own
Olympic appearance – no mean feat.

Before her professional woman's tour,
before endorsements, Billie Jean King returned
Court's volley with a forceful backhand
and character challenges which continue.

I remember Heartland legislators
raised the floor – no extramural girls' sports!
"Could damage girls' reproductive organs."
Court would check a locker room gaze as sinful.

On different sides of an Australian civil rights hearing,
Billie Jean rose, then rose again. Her serve preceded her.
This King loomed, a public figure, a role model. Each
taught us pride in excellence, to play to win.

The circle dial of a diamond Movado.
The arch support of a top athletic shoe.
The glossy green 4-color fashion campaign.
Brand names embrace the Union Jack's snap.

Now watch grand slam champion Venus Williams,
strained by chronic illness. Her arms fall, failing
weary too soon, far away from Center Court,
yet returning again and again.

THREE POEMS AFTER THE JAZZ OF NICOLE MITCHELL

1.

"Meadow Sunlight in the Swinging Field"

We think of a soprano flute
As something light – BUTTERFLIES
Lighter than air
And its flutist – under the sun
Rarely a first chair – BUTTERFLIES.

But keep in the back of your mind
BUTTERFLIES
See B R E A T H = L I F E.
Nicole contracts – under her sun
And releases her breath to fly,
hold and reach every
ensemble member
and they reach her, reaching.

Whether the "idiomatic logic that goes on" in her
or Joni's head
allows her students to follow – BUTTERFLIES
But never simply imitate her – sun down.
Or is she a teacher who allows her listeners to sing or
urges her students to fly on their own.

There is that pedestrian art – and BUTTERFLIES
And those airs that limn the marvelous sun.

https://youtu.be/Rdson8DIdGs [Y Link}Ru
Nicole Mitchell's Black Earth Ensemble, "Meadow Sunlight in
the Swinging Fields."

2.

Indigi Trio – Nicole Mitchell Solo Flute

Grasshopper in black leather sings
In the dead of night.
Take this sound and push it to the end

Of my fancy. Far into the waking day
Jumping till no piercers find a place
To name land.
Grasshopper in black leather sings

In the dead of night.
Here here here I am.
Come catch me.

Indigi Trio – Nicole Mitchell Solo Flute
https://youtu.be/uuL2CNYXyMc

3.

Sonic Projections

Vision Festival, Roulette, Brooklyn
14 June 2014

It is as if somebody's moving
Heavy furniture into a tiny apartment
The acoustic piano breaks in.
Put. That. There.

A tuft of red against thick brown wool tweed.

That touch of sound.
The chaos roars back.
Her rough lyrical intervention matches
Growl for growl.
The quartet's leader sways in flip flops.
Urging, prodding, coaxing, and stomping out a sound.
Lifting it high above her head.

That rough lyricism again.
Good dark chocolate
Laced with red peppers.

"Sonic Projections"
https://youtu.be/t8ae6FkWK4k

Lyrics for Maria
A Sequence in Seven Parts

1.

Fried Eggs in Butter

Time to wake you up,
cook us fried eggs in butter
fresh black pepper and rosemary
for remembrance.
My iron skillet stays cold.

2.

Haiku

Let them go, the rain-
soaked petals on the path.
In time, cover the roots.

3.

Things Overheard in the Neighborhood — An Answer Poem

Stay away from the Jamaicans;
they own property
and drive cabs.

OK man!
Drop the keys!
Why?
Just drop the keys, man.

I don't know if
you said what
I think you just said, but
if you did, you just damn
wish you never said it.

Hey Mami! – amplified
by three pairs of beloved
young-boy eyes.

Got blunts?

4.

DIRTY RED PARKA

Tonight, an exuberant man
in a dirty red parka
sat down next to me
in the Kitchen.
How's the chicken?
Great!
He said his mother finally
got through from Puerto Rico
this morning, 7:30 AM
after 3 weeks.
Son, she asked, *When
are you planning
to get married?*
But Mother. I am married.
To my husband.
*Son, if you are happy
I am happy.*

5.

AMORE OR LESS

Love in the subbasement?
Cement, not hardwood floors?
No broad planks of oak?
Too much is plenty.

The love hungry never travel
on their bellies.
Can windows be louvered
at the sidewalk?

No isinglass panels hang
in mahogany frames.
We know we have no crystal stair.
Amore or less are we.

Can sheets and pillows be
laid down just right
so as never to be subject to eviction,
foreclosure or property tax abduction?

What we long for vs. what we have –
when I open my door, would you
stand in its frame?

6.

Resilience

Clear a space now
Clear a space now
Clear a space so
You can move.
Walk to the middle of the floor.

Contract. Release. Risk off-center
(Daily, keep finding your center
and strengthening that core.)

Fall down on purpose, Monkey Face
– take care for the slivers
from the old oak floor.
Or did they grease our floor?

Fall again. Fall again. Fall again. Fall.
Until the people cannot rise.

7.

Haiku

The dawn rises now
impatient with desire.
As if we won, plant roses.

SONG FOR STARS AND WILD GRASS

"Flowers came to mind for some reason.

"Our train plunges on through the pitch-black night,
I never knew I liked the night pitch black
Sparks fly from the engine
I didn't know I loved sparks
I didn't know I loved so many things and I had to wait until sixty
to find it out sitting by that window on the Prague-Berlin train
watching the world disappear as if on a journey of no return."
"Things I Didn't Know I Loved" Nâzim Hikmet (19 April 1962)
                                                                    Moscow

Ten fingers over a rough palm. Blue clouds cloaked black night
and its wash of fresh stars. Fingers once ever limber,
hesitate over a piano keyboard.
Grasses beneath a mill flora galaxy grow in all their varieties
Yellow mesa flowers with spots of periwinkle and red.
A generous, detailed expanse, ignored. Step away. How many
different grasses can you count?

I didn't know I loved correspondences.
That prairie in Illinois, this grassland in New Mexico.
Here, I expect Barbara Stanwick to mosey on by,
but it's only Taylor Swift
regretting her lost virginity, lost to a MUSICIAN, no less.
But this vendor of crystals would do Barbara proud,
her leathery skin and fascination
with everybody's story. She'd quarried her own gems
and moved them herself,
with time to attend an esoteric knowledge seminar.

I didn't know I loved collecting stories to bring home:
short,
shaggy dog,
some almost true.
I didn't remember I loved lives with difference and silken ties.

First an inaugural gathering with no personal contacts.
From my own train, needing a local bus
toward the airport shuttle, one driver barked "Wrong line."
Couldn't I see that this was a G
and I clearly needed an E route? Actually, no
I'd just arrived in ABQ from ORD on a bus-free Sunday.
A plaza of total strangers. Would they find me strange?
Would poems built on an Acer
stand proudly next to ones from a Mitsubishi?
Would everybody have cuter leggings at yoga?

Would the ghost of Georgia O'Keefe rise up
and demand a favorite image sketched at
the Art Institute of Chicago, or be deported back to iron skies
over Lake Michigan?

A Man Walked into Our "El" Car

A stocky man with a salt-n-pepper brush cut walked into our "El" car yesterday from the next car, carrying an Anonymous mask and wearing fake sheriff stars. I was reading a new book about Latinas, the media and citizenship. He entered the space where the doors open, and held up a battered tablet, after slowly putting on his mask. *Great. Socially engaged performance artists are the new mimes.* He started circling and taking pictures of the passengers, then sat down directly opposite me. I firmly told him to stop taking my picture without permission. I was a member of SAG-AFTRA, and held up my newly paid-up membership card, and added that he did not have my permission to shoot. That I had rights. He started screaming at me. I asked if he had a problem with immigrants. He continued to scream, and shouted from behind his mask that I needed to go back to wherever I came from – that he was a REAL AMERICAN. I blandly said I was born here, in Chicago. NO! NO YER NOT! I refrained from offering this loud mime an American history nugget that folks who looked like me all became U.S. citizens in 1917. He still kept screaming, but by now was also still texting furiously. He grunted that I was fairly photogenic, though. The guy sitting next to me just had a half smile, and continued his Candy Crush game, occasionally looking up at the masked man. As I rose to exit, I calmly called Anonymous a privileged, entitled prick.

◊◊◊

A Safer Place

If you asked politely, the police could send you to an emergency shelter, a "safe place" if you had nowhere else to go and didn't want to spend the night under a tree. Your prayers would be ushered into lock step, as so many sardonic riffs on "Amazing Grace," that freedom song, rang out from the back rows of nightly prayer service.

In this shelter, the men were said to have been just released. The women seemed traumatized, with few resources except those within the criminal justice system. I have spent time in state psychiatric hospitals, for mood swings. This topped any and all dayrooms. Sometimes meds were locked up and not dispensed, or stolen while locked away. Praise Jesus! Half of city mental health clinics and most in-patient facilities were suddenly closed. This shelter had a mission to accept everybody, but had few trained psych or medical aides. No one seemed able to pull aside and calm an agitated "overnight guest." Once, I sat waiting for the showers, after an evening prayer service. A young woman politely excused herself before throwing up into her toiletries bag. Her meds for manic depression had been changed that day, she explained. We sat together. She smiled and said, "Thank you. God is great." No one on the staff blinked.

You might catch the eye of a night matron, shower under the eye of another matron, and hand over your street clothes to a "hot box," to kill any bedbugs. If you needed to leave early for work or a program, your clothes were hung on an open rack. Upstairs, above my towel, my pink surgical scar was noted by some. They looked and nodded, looked down, and backed away. It was my warrior tattoo.

Bureaucracy had its needs, and the Department of Human Services (DHS) and the Chicago Housing Authority (CHA, under the federal Department of Housing and Urban Development or HUD) required a "Homeless Letter (roof/no roof)." At the community service center, I spent 15 minutes listening to an explanation as to why there is no such letter. If it existed, it would be worthless. How would he know if indeed, I was homeless? Is he expected to verify that I live at this particular shelter? He could only verify with a reasonable degree of certainty that I said that I live at this shelter. If such a letter even existed. I shifted in my seat, my lower back stiff from 8 days of sleeping on the concrete floor of the overfull, yet hypothetical, shelter. The HUD form required this pro forma letter. Finally, he sighed and reached across his desk to his desktop forms file, and pulled a blank "HOMELESS LETTER" form, filled it out in seconds, then asked if I needed a second copy.

I had been referred back to him by an agency administrator, who took my call by accident, thinking that I was one of her caseworkers. She insisted that her agency no longer provided homeless letters. She put me on hold, then sent me back to the community service center, the office which provides access to current information on city and state programs. And the HUD housing application, to place my name in the subsidized housing voucher lottery or an annual building waitlist? They lost my application. Sorry. Try again in six months.

Transitional housing was more likely if one was transitioning from a shelter. I landed an ongoing tutoring gig, leaving from the day shelter. From a transitional women's shelter, there was lobbying downstate for homeless support, and a phone bank job which I lost after forgetting my passwords each day, and listening too long to lonely seniors outside of the day's demos. A shelter resident accused me of punching her in her face. I was sternly told that violence was not acceptable, and I was given 40 minutes to pack. Friends offered dinners, solitary showers, and a safe place to sleep for a few days. Once in a safer place, it was easier to navigate the various bureaucracies and the job search, and check mail at the currency exchange. If only I could draft the right list. I dreamt of floors falling through. There were several moments of grace over the three years, but salvation would mean fundamental change and a stable income.

Finally a solid break, a retail job on salary and commission. The owner thought I would be good selling upscale shoes to barefoot matrons. A co-worker realized where I went home each night, and dropped word to her landlord. Soon enough, an empty month-to-month two-bedroom in Bridgeport was mine. My ESL student, a Catholic deacon and plant supervisor, had his sessions with me cut off, but not before he handed me an envelope as a housewarming gift – money to buy a bed.

Reunited, my feline duchess settled into our new home, after her own "temporary safer place" had caught fire. She insisted that all doors be left open, and pawed them open one by one. She cried out at 3 AM. I stumbled after her through the kitchen, passing her empty bowls. Two squares of streetlight colored the dark wood floor of the near empty front room. She calmly spread herself across one of the squares, looked at me perched on the love seat, and purred loudly. Here we are.

My new keys seem to replicate: the key for the downstairs outside door (locked at night); a key for the back apartment entrance (deadbolt and doorknob); a key for the front entrance (deadbolt and doorknob); a key for the storage locker; a key for the mailbox at the currency exchange. Then there are the three keys which might just be old keys – but you never know.

I was born in Chicago's Englewood neighborhood, and grew up in the southwest suburbs. Since 1978, I had had a series of studios on the North Side. The mailbox keys worked in the lobbies. Then, with hard times and a weekly status at a single room occupancy hotel, I could keep my key and its green fob on my basin, rather than at the front desk. These new keys could be so easily taken back. "Focus forward," suggests a gentle friend, spotting the panic behind my eyes.

The speaker in the store started to call me bad names. It was hard to tell if someone was talking to me, or if it was a voice inside.

I lost that job four months into the new place – no severance, unemployment, or back commissions. I kept slipping, and there was no ice on the ground, just alternate legs collapsing. I landed on smooth concrete sidewalks downtown as I tried to keep up. I could see my closed door from here. Salvation began with a Social Security disability hearing officer, who said that I have a strong work ethic, and deemed me unfit to work. "You kept getting back up," she said. The call about her decision came at my last SRO, which later shut down in favor of renovation to upscale studios. I cried out and wept, reassured the caller I was OK, then began packing.

THE DAYS OF BOBBY'S PASSING

It was my favorite month in a good year. I'd just turned 13, and looked forward to one more year of St. Benedict's before the adventures of Dwight D. Eisenhower Community High School. I was stretched out on a blanket in our backyard, fingering some Scrabble® tiles. My mother, my married cousin Arlene and I had just finished a game. We had been giggling and arguing over some words that my mother insisted were too new to be in the dictionary. Mom and Arlene lingered over the argument, and sipped martinis from glass tumblers. Neither Arlene nor Mom wanted to go worry over dinner. Maybe we could talk our old men into ordering pizza, suggested Arlene.

Was the breeze really starting to get sharp? The shadows were longer, and I was sitting in part of a tree shape, instead of a pool of sun. The mosquitoes teased the backs of my calves, but no little bumps were on my skin.

WCFL blared out top 40 hits. The DJ's commentary tossed out between the rock & roll somehow stilled all of us. "We all killed him," he declared. "Not just Sirhan Sirhan pulled the trigger on Bobby Kennedy. First JFK, then Martin Luther King, Jr., Watts, Viet Nam, the Convention – our whole, violent gun-happy society cut young Senator Robert F. Kennedy down."

My mother got up to make more martinis – reaching for the Tupperware® pitcher, slowly crossing the yard, the driveway, up the back steps. The screen door creaked open, wheezed and clicked shut.

We have a wooden, not aluminum, back door in May of 1961. My dad's older brother opens it and calls out, "Come here. I wanna show you something." I am 5, and seriously molding the driveway cinders into a little town, while supervising my

almost-4-year-old brother Gary. We have been careful to stay
out of our Nonnie's peony patch alongside the drive. Now what?

We trudge up the stairs. Uncle Art goes inside, and now comes
back. Our Nonnie is saying something, first pleading then
yelling in Italian. He opens the door and shows us both a
shiny shotgun. As he lowers the barrel to Gary's right ear, he
looks up and asks me, "Do you wanna see something?"

I look up at his eyes, his greasy slicked-back black hair, the
shotgun. It can't be loaded, I think, informed by scenes from
Gunsmoke.

"Yes," I reply.

A sound like God exploding goes off next to my feet. Gary is in
a heap, his head like a saint's, in a round stain as red as his
favorite cap, the sailor cap with earflaps and a chinstrap.

I run screaming upstairs – "Mommy! Mommy! Something's
happened to Gary" – running back downstairs with Momma.

She cries out for him, for me – "Don't go! Don't go!"
"I gotta get help! I gotta get help!" I keep on running, across
the backyard and alley to the door of my mother's best friend,
Katie.

"Call the police," she tells her daughter. "Stay here," were her
very last words to me, and I did.

I look through a bedroom window with Janice, over to the
small bench below our back porch. My mother is cradling my
little brother, rocking him, her cheek smeared with blood.
"Why is Mommy bleeding? Did she kiss Gary?" No answer.

As a college student, a traveling buddy and I had been
having too much fun to leave the hilltop Coca-Cola stand
near the Vatican. In the half-hour left of that Sunday
afternoon, we went right to the important sights: the Sistine

Chapel, the Vatican Post Office, and St. Peter's Basilica. In St. Peter's, set into a side chapel, was Michelangelo's Pieta. In flawless marble chiseled smooth, an ageless Mary held her broken Son across her lap, hands turned down. Somehow, the marble revealed her misery without a single drop a blood.

The DJ said in conclusion, "Aren't we then all responsible for the assassination of RFK?"

My chills were gone now. "No," I whispered.

[Note: Only my mother survived her head wounds. For the three shootings, my uncle served 25 years in a state criminal mental health facility. He never went to trial. He died alone in a locked VA hospital ward, his own voices stilled.]

– Finis –

ACKNOWLEDGMENTS AND PREVIOUS PUBLICATIONS

CHAPBOOKS

Ceremonies. Chicago: dancing girl press, 2014.

Debris: Poems and Memoir. Arlington Hts.: Moon Journal Press, November 2005. Reprinted and redesigned 2011 by Puddin'head Press.

PRINT ANTHOLOGIES

Hidden Screams: An Anthology of Violence Against Girls and Young Women. Ed. Santosh Bakaya and Lopamudra Banerjee. Authorspress, New Delhi, 2019.

The Current. Ed. Sreena Mudgerer. Karala, India, 2019.

The Hestler Street Fair Anthology. Ed. Azriel Johnson. Writing Knights, Cleveland, 2019.

EXTREME: an anthology for social and environmental justice. Ed. Mark Lipman. Vagabond, Venice, CA 2018.

RISE: an anthology of Unity and Power. Ed. Mark Lipman. Vagabond, Venice, CA, 2017.

Overthrowing Capitalism vols. II, IV, V, VI. Revolutionary Poets Brigade: San Francisco, Ed. Jack Hirschman, Agneta Falk and John Curl. Kallatumba Press. 2016-2019.

Cantologia: Amor. Ed. Miguel Lopez Lemus. Guild Complex, Chicago. 2016.

The Significant Anthology. Ed. Ampat Koshy and Reena Presad. Jaipour, India, 2015.

Breaking Mirrors/Raw Images. Ed. Felicia Sue Kaplan. (4:30 Poets, Chicago)

The Muse for World Peace: An Anthology of Contemporary Poets Propagating World Peace. Ed. Mutiu Olawuyi, compiled by Gabriel Timileyin Olajuwon. (Gambia, 2015)

Between the Heart and the Land/Entre el corázon y la tierra: Latina Poets in the Midwest. Eds. Brenda Cardenas and Johanny Vazquez Paz. MARCH/Abrazo Press, Chicago, 2001.

ALTERNATIVE MEDIA

Love You Madly. Online jazz poetry project curated by Lisa Alvarado, Santa Fe, 2016.

Eclectica Magazine @eclectica.org. October 2017.

LaBloga @labloga.blogspot.com reposted 5 poems from "Poets Responding to SB 1070" (Facebook page). "Asylum" appeared in *LaBloga's* "Best of 2014" issue.

Caravel webzine/*The People's Tribune.com, 2017.*

Book of Voices @Voices.e-poets.net/MarinoE. Critical essay and portfolio, curated by Kurt Heinz, 2002.

LITTLE MAGAZINES (Print)

After Hours Magazine (Chicago); *Nit & Wit* (Chicago).

Thank you to my editor, Mark Lipman, who saw that socially engaged and lyric need not be mutually exclusive, and worth collaborative effort with this aging provocateur. Also thanks to New Town Writers, for their thoughtful feedback to an allegedly cis female.

Some of these poems began at the Las Dos Brujas Writers' Workshop, on the Ghost Ranch, Albiquiu, New Mexico. The grant which supported my attendance was a Community Arts Assistance Project grant from the City of Chicago Department of Cultural Affairs and Special Events and the Illinois Arts Council, a state agency. Thank you Christina Garcia and Juan Felipe Herrera.

Biography

Chicago poet Elizabeth Marino has seen her work travel. Her poems and essays have appeared in little magazines, litzines, blogs and print anthologies in India, Gambia, England, Scotland, San Francisco, Austin, Cleveland and Chicago, including two Vagabond collections (*Rise* and *EXTREME*). Prior releases include two chapbooks, *Debris* (Puddin'head Press, 2011) and *Ceremonies* (dancing girl press 2016). She was awarded a Ragdale residency, a Hispanic Serving Institution grant, and a CAAP grant. She holds an MA in English from University of Illinois at Chicago's Writers Program and a BA in English and Humanities from Barat College, in addition to coursework at the University of Oxford. She earned her living teaching writing and literature at local universities for years, as well as had a popular SAGE workshop.

VAGABOND